Surrender your Struggles to God

family bills illness job rejection

LEESA KING

Copyright © 2022 by Leesa King.

ISBN: 978-1-957009-24-7 (sc)
ISBN: 978-1-957009-25-4 (e)

Library of Congress Control Number: 2022902618

All rights reserved. No part of this book may be reproduced, stored, or transmitted by any means—whether auditory, graphic, mechanical, or electronic—without written permission of both publisher and author, except in the case of brief excerpts used in critical articles and reviews. Unauthorized reproduction of any part of this work is illegal and is punishable by law.

My prayer as you read this book is that you realize no matter what our struggle is, God is always with us. No matter our life choices, we can always ask for help or forgiveness. God will provide for us. God wants us to have a relationship with Him through prayer, talking with Him, reading His word, and enjoying the company of other believers. God can use you. He has provided each of us with certain talents, abilities, and gifts that can be used to help others in their time of need.

> "For I know the plans I have for you," says the Lord.
> "They are plans for good and not for disaster to
> give you a future and a hope" (Jer. 29:11, NLT).

Have you ever looked back on your life and wondered how you arrived here today? How you've made it through situations that you never thought you'd go through? Or things/situations that happened to your parents? For me it's amazing, it is only through God that I am here today.

My mother states that her parents thought she would die in infancy. Today, we would describe it as failure to thrive. My grandmother did everything the doctor told her, but nothing helped. They took pictures of mother so they would remember her. Grandmother decided to try cow's milk, and amazingly, my mother started to gain weight. When the doctor visited (yes, once upon a time, doctors did make house calls), he was surprised. The doctor asked grandmother what she was doing. She responded that she was giving her baby cow's milk.

"Are you trying to kill her?"

"I've done everything you told me and nothing worked. I tried cow's milk and see, she is doing well."

God gives us answers in many ways. Do people actually hear God's voice verbally? Some may, most people will receive thoughts, or God will have someone tell you what you need to know. God has also given His word, the Bible, to guide us. The Lord guided my grandmother to use what was on hand at the farm—cow's milk. My mother is currently eighty-five years old.

Mother worked as a telephone operator both before and after I was born. Mom states that the operators would check on the elderly in the community. If someone called and sound confused they would contact a family member to go check on the person. My grandmother and a lady named Mrs. Warner would watch me. When I was nine years old mom took a job at the drug store. The arrangement was she worked on days that dad was home. My father was a fireman and was at the fire department for twenty-four hours, then home; that way we always had a parent home. (Mother's parents passed away before I was eight years old. My father's parents had passed before I was born).

Mom demonstrated her love in many ways. My first seizure occurred when I was three years old. I was hospitalized. My mother told me the staff encouraged her to go home for the night. She said she needed to be with me. They had her go to the waiting room for a while. I woke up and didn't see her. I said, "I want my mommy." "She's not here." "I want my mommy" - over and over, louder and louder. Finally, a nurse allowed my mother to stay the night with me. Mom said when I woke I would see her, be satisfied and return to sleep. Hospitals today recognize the security needs children have and provide nice recliners in patient rooms.

When I was seven I became a brownie scout. Mom was the assistant leader with my aunt, then she became leader in my second year. The brownie troop met in our basement. I remember at Thanksgiving or Christmas time, mom had us make little gifts using toilet paper rolls. We wrapped green crepe paper over the rolls, filled the rolls with hard candies and tie a ribbon on it. Then we went to a nursing home to visit the clients and give them the candy gifts.

Mom enjoyed sewing. One year she made costumes for the church's Christmas program, shepherds, angels and wise men. She made crowns from plastic bottles and spray painted them. Our church used those costumes for many years.

Mom went to work full-time when my brother started school. She worked night shift as the switchboard operator/admissions clerk at the local hospital.

My father was a marine in World War II, fighting in the Pacific. One of the battles my father participated in was the Battle of Guadalcanal where 1,600 Americans were killed, 4,200 wounded, several thousand died from malaria and other tropical diseases (Encyclopedia Britannica).

The Lord's hand was upon my father, he contracted malaria and was in the hospital in Australia. A doctor told Dad that he only had a few days to live, he was asked, "Would you be willing to try an experimental medicine?"

My father agreed. The medicine worked. He made it through the war, met my mother, and married. Dad was a firefighter for the federal government and a wonderful, caring father until he went home to be with the Lord at the age of sixty-one. I'm looking forward to seeing Daddy again!

Without the Lord's hand being upon my parents, protecting them, my brother and I wouldn't be here. Thank you, Lord, for my parents. I believe my desire to help others was in large part due to my parents caring for and helping others, even in their career choices.

My father was tall and kind. All of the neighborhood boys would try to dunk Dad in the community pool, but they never could. He was always there. Dad came home from work one day when I had a seizure at the age of nine. I felt better knowing nothing would hurt me because Daddy was there. It is the same type of faith and trust our Lord wants us to have in Him. He is Daddy! No matter what we go through, He is there. If someone hurts us physically or emotionally, tell God your feelings including anger toward Him. What is hard is that people have free will and some choose to hurt us; also, we've lived in a fallen world since Adam and Eve ate of the tree of knowledge. We now suffer from illnesses as part of our life process. Talk to God. The Lord will let us try to solve problems or resolve situations on our own until we come to a point of frustration or run into a wall. When we ask Him, the Lord will guide us. The Lord is our creator and He loves us. The Lord wants us to follow Him and be obedient to His word. When we fail to do so, we suffer consequences, but He always forgives us when we come to Him.

I grew up in a rural mountain area. Our first house was on a busy street. We lived next door to a grocery store. I remember trying to get the gumball with a stripe from the gumball machine. If you got the striped gumball, you won a candy bar. My mother tells the story when I was very young, under five years of age, when I swallowed the gumball and started choking. Mother stated there were three other ladies in the store and everyone froze. She picked me up, turned me upside down, and out came the gumball. I put it back in my mouth and started choking. Again, Mom turned me upside down, out came the gumball. I don't think I was allowed gumballs for a while after that incident.

Another time of possible death was when I was six years old. It was winter. We had snow in piles on the side of the road. I walked to the bus stop in front of the store. A man was driving his car on the street and almost didn't see me, but he saw my bright stocking cap moving as I walked. This time the Lord protected me with a stocking cap. Amazing how something simple, and we may think insignificant, protected my life. God uses everyday things, everyday people, to help us; not just protecting us, but growing in many ways, learning new things, understanding more about His love for us, and in helping others.

But even during this time, God was there. My mother was scared for my life, the other ladies too and they froze not knowing what to do. God gave my mother the ability to turn me upside down and prevented my death. She explained to me later in my life that she panicked after the incident was over, but God saw us through.

We moved to a new home when I was seven years old. We had lots of trees in our yard and woods behind our house. My father and a teenage neighbor built us a treehouse complete with a roof and ladder to climb up on. My parents had an old kitchen table and chairs they put in the treehouse. We had a small neighborhood, but many days, the children would come over to play where we would swing on the tire swing, climb trees, and walk in the woods. We attended school in town along with other surrounding communities.

I was diagnosed with hypothyroidism in high school. I had nodules on the thyroid that hemorrhaged and had surgery to remove the nodules. My vocal cords suffered trauma from the surgery. I spoke in a whisper for four months. Definitely traumatic to a seventeen-year-old girl. I remember one day in sociology class, the teacher asked a question and I was the only person to raise my hand to answer. The teacher stated, "Doesn't anyone else know the answer? I don't want to hear her talk." I realized later that the teacher thought it was best to rest my voice, but I felt rejection at the time. As a teenager I was very self-conscious of my surgery scar. After my voice came back I resumed teaching Sunday school. One Sunday I overheard one girl say to another "Miss Leesa has two smiles." That statement touched my heart and I received some emotional healing.

Pastor Wayne stated in a Wednesday evening prayer and Bible study that for most people, it takes their adolescent and some adult years to decide on a career. Others know by the time they are in kindergarten. I'm one of those. I've always wanted to be a nurse. It may have been from the time I was in the hospital over Christmas at age of three, or that an aunt and an older cousin were nurses. I enjoyed listening to my cousin tell stories of being a nurse in World War II, during family reunions. When the neighborhood children decided to play army, I was the nurse who fixed them up; and of course, I read books about Florence Nightingale and Clara Barton. My journey to obtaining my RN was emotional, at times wondering if I would ever achieve that goal.

I was the tallest girl in my class. There was a certain cartoon in my late elementary years about King Kong, because of my height the boys would call me King Kong. My parents would say, "Ignore that," but I didn't know how. My self-esteem became low through the years—junior high school into high school. In junior high (now called middle school), I felt like I really didn't belong, but I did have a few friends. High school was better. I made friends from the other side of town, but I was definitely not one of the popular students. I studied. Before the advent of community service for high schoolers was a requirement, I did community service. Ninth and tenth grade, I volunteered after school at the daycare center; junior and senior years, I was a candy striper. The hospital taught us some basics such as vital signs, bathing patients, and making beds. I participated in Future Nurses Club, Girls Glee Club, and Bible Study. But in eleventh grade, I made a new friend who was a minister's daughter. She stated, "Jesus died for you. You are equal to everyone else. You are not less than anyone."

That statement hit me as truth, but it took years before I accepted that God gave me certain talents/abilities, and I can do things; if other people put me down, I don't need to accept that as my truth.

If your child is being teased or bullied at school, please talk with your child's teacher and principal. Tell them you expect their intervention when situations occur. You may need to keep a journal of the incidents—time, date, what happened, what preceded the incident, any other students involved? Any adults around? This can help your school by showing areas where they can improve their vigilance. Encourage your child to talk with you or another trusted adult. Encourage your child to be with friends, not alone when possible. Let your child know how special he/she is. Focus on their strengths and interests. Have them get involved with outside activities such as scouts, sports, music, and art. Help them develop a list of their good qualities, abilities, skills. They are not what someone else calls them.

If your child becomes anxious, withdrawn, doesn't want to go to school, please consider seeing a counselor (schools provide guidance counselors), to help your child express what is happening, how they are feeling, and ways to cope.

I was accepted into a three-year nursing program that had all the college classes plus nursing (today they split it up or encourage you to take the college classes before the nursing classes). On the first day, an instructor said, "Look to your left, look to your right, one of the three of you will be gone in December." This was very scary. I failed microbiology. It was the first time I ever failed a class. I went home depressed. I did take classes at the community college and returned to the nursing program the following fall. I took microbiology again from the same professor. I managed to get a C in the class. That was the hardest C I ever got. Then I did not pass clinical. Clinical was the skills part of our training, working with patients. I was anxious and it definitely showed. I wanted to do the skills perfectly—dressing changes, catheterizations, etc. I felt scrutinized by some instructors, and pressured myself for perfection. Beginning any undertaking, you are not going to be perfect.

Part of the drive to be perfect in performing tasks is that we think we will not receive criticism. But no matter what we do, or how we do the job/task, some people will find something wrong. We need to realize we are always learning in some manner. Sometimes criticism is constructive, sometimes hurtful or embarrassing. After your initial response to a criticism, take time to step back and look at it and your response to the criticism. Is there some truth to it? Are your feelings of hurt, disappointment, failure, or not measuring up more than what was intended in the situation? Sometimes we are responding to something that happened to us years ago. Pray about your situation, talk with a friend or trusted coworker. If you are finding yourself taking things harder emotionally, perhaps there is an imbalance within your body. I have hypothyroidism. If my blood level is not within normal limits, I become more emotional and depressed. If you are experiencing stress in your life—situations within your family or finances—this contributes to your reaction. If the person involved is a supervisor or coworker, consider talking to that person. If talking with them is not effective, then consider talking with your human resource department. Another option may be that it is time to move on to another job. Pray for guidance, don't make any hasty decisions. The Lord will help you and show you what you need. Also, as difficult as it is, we are to pray for others including those who hurt us. They may be going through difficulties that we are unaware of.

After failing clinical, I decided to attend the college, got a degree in a related field, therapeutic recreation with a minor in psychology. I went to a bible study off campus held at an art professor's house. I met several people who invited me to a Christian coffeehouse then to church. For me, my college years was a time of learning and growing in the Lord. Yes, I grew up in a church, Presbyterian. Yes, I was in children's choir, took communicant's class at age thirteen, and taught Sunday school. I prayed. But I remember sitting in church one day saying, "Is this all there is to Christianity?" If you ask that question, the Lord will show you that there is more, much more in knowing Him.

The Lord led me to a church that had a pastor who preached from all of the Bible as well as having a mix of hymns with contemporary worship songs. I joined the staff at the coffeehouse serving drinks (non-alcoholic of course) and snacks before the musicians' sets and during their break, making popcorn for the tables. I also taught children's church. I stayed in that city for about eighteen months after graduation. I worked two jobs and was laid off. I moved back home with my parents, got a job and went to a different nursing program. I drove forty-five minutes to school, paid my way and this time made it through, praise God! Being older when I started the program made a difference. I was more mature and had most of the required college courses prior to beginning the program. I even helped other students who were struggling with their studies. I took the state board exam, which at that time was a two-day event. I waited for the results, going to the post office every day for several weeks until my aunt who was the post mistress called and said, "There is an envelope here addressed to Leesa King, RN." Woo-hoo! Thank you, Lord! One week after I returned home from college, I went to church only to return to find my father on his knees on the floor, talking on the phone with my mother. He was in pain. I drove him to the hospital. After tests, it was discovered that Dad had kidney cancer. He had surgery to remove the kidney, and radiation therapy. I was there to help him and take him to his therapy sessions that were back in my old college town. Dad did well and returned to work. After nursing school, I got a job in Virginia, at a state mental health hospital. However, after moving there, we discovered Dad's cancer had returned. He retired from his firefighting job. I drove four and a half hours to my home anytime I had two or more days off to spend with Dad. The last time I went home, Dad was in the hospital. He had cloth restraints on his wrists to prevent him from getting out of bed on his own as he was so weak he could fall. Seeing my dad in this condition was very difficult. I left the room and went to the shopping center. I sat on a bench thinking about my father. Two different friends came across me. Both prayed with me. My prayer was that the Lord would take Dad home soon and that I would be there. This prayer was answered the next day. Mother and I were with him. I was feeding Dad beef broth and grape juice (his favorite) with a big syringe. I turned to get more juice, when I turned back he was gone. I said, "Mom, he's gone."

A nurse came in and stated, "Oh, he stops breathing sometimes." I said, "No, Dad's gone." And he was.

Later, seeing Dad in his casket, he looked very peaceful. I knew Dad was happy being with our Lord, no more pain or fatigue. But I do miss him and look forward to the day when I will see him again. I still cry every time I share this story.

A good friend called me a week after the funeral. Nancy realized I was probably withdrawing in my grief. She told me, "I'm coming to pick you up, we're going out to dinner then see a movie." I tried to say no, but Nancy told me she would see me in thirty minutes and for me to "be ready." She's a good friend, I needed that before returning back to work. Friends are blessings from God.

After returning to Virginia, I had difficulty handling church. We would sing and I would cry. I felt closer to Dad knowing he was with God and being in the services, I missed him more. It took close to a year before I was able to sit through an entire service without crying. God understands. Grieving is a long process. For most people, it takes six months to four years to grieve a loved one (familydoctor.org). But even after that amount of time, you may experience grief in some manner, especially on the anniversary of the person's death, or their birthday, or during the holidays.

Elizabeth Kubler-Ross wrote in her book *On Death and Dying* that there are five stages of grief: (1) denial and isolation, (2) anger, (3) bargaining, (4) depression, (5) and acceptance. Many people move back and forth between these stages before reaching the acceptance stage. During our grieving process, we need to remember that God is always with us. Isaiah 41:10 (NLT) states, "Don't be afraid, for I am with you. Don't be discouraged, for I am your God. I will strengthen you and help you. I will hold you up with my victorious right hand."

We also grieve when we lose other things. According to helpguide.org, the list can include the following: (1) divorce or relationship breakup, (2) loss of health, (3) losing a job, (4) loss of financial stability, (5) a miscarriage, (6) retirement, (7) death of a pet, (8 loss of a cherished dream, (9) a loved one's serious illness, (10) loss of a friendship, (11) loss of safety after a trauma, (12) and selling the family home.

Grieving stages:
1. Denial: you may feel numb or shocked upon the death of a loved one. It's hard to believe you will not be able to talk with them again. Even when you are expecting the death of a loved one who is terminally ill, when the death occurs, you still experience the numbness or shock.
2. Anger: you may feel angry with yourself, perhaps your last encounter with the person was a while ago, or you had an argument. You may be angry that you did not spend more time with the person. You may feel guilt or you may feel anger toward the doctors or with God that your loved one died.
3. Bargaining: trying to make a deal with God.
4. Depression: sadness, fatigue, loss of appetite or eating more, not sleeping well. This is all part of the grief process. Allow yourself to go through these emotions. Find friends or family to talk about your loved one, how you feel now. Cry or find another outlet for your emotions. Please do not try to numb the feelings by turning to alcohol. The feelings will still be there, it is better to express them in some way.
5. Acceptance: you have accepted that your loved one is no longer here on earth to turn to. You can continue in your life of going to work, interacting with family and friends. But you may find, even years from now, experiencing some sadness when you think about your loved one.

As you've read, I experience sadness and tears when I tell the story of my dad's passing even thirty-two years after his going home to be with God. That is another thing that may help you. Picture your loved one in heaven, no more pain or sorrow. You will see them again, you are separated temporarily, not forever. My cat, Nikki, passed away at the age of eighteen. She was my baby. Nikki was a small cat that I took in as a stray kitten in Georgia. She was a very sweet cat. The last three years of her life, I took her to the vet twice a week to receive fluids under her skin (subcutaneous) to help her kidneys function. One day, she stopped eating. I took Nikki back to the vet, she told me that Nikki's liver was failing and she would pass in two to three days. I decided to have her put to sleep the next evening. I gave her lots of love, wrapped Nikki in her blanket, and went to the vet's. My mother drove the car. The vet gave Nikki the first injection to make her sleep. At that time I prayed to the Lord to take her to himself. I even had a little bottle of olive oil and anointed my cat. Some people may think that is a little crazy, but it was a comfort to me. The vet gave Nikki the injection that stopped her heart. It took only seconds. She was gone. I cried. I'm crying now as I write this story. I did not take in another cat for years, not until I moved into my own house and been there for over a year.

One late afternoon after work, I arrived in my driveway to a sound of loud mewling. There was a small black and white kitten who was lost. My neighbor and I got her, fed her, wrapped the kitten up in a towel. I called Mom to ask for the cat carrier. She brought it to me. I took the kitten to the emergency veterinary clinic thirty minutes away. They checked her out, no rabies, distemper, or feline leukemia. They gave the kitten her initial vaccinations. Then I took the kitten to my own vet a few days later. I hadn't planned on getting another cat, but here she was. The kitten would climb my drapes, she was getting into all kinds of trouble, so I named her Lucy. Now Lucy is four years old and has calmed down. She likes to play fetch with rubber bands. I'm glad Lucy is in my life.

Pamela (not her real name) was a good friend for over twelve years. We met at work back in the mid-1990s. She moved to our area from New York City where her family immigrated from the Caribbean. Pamela met a man she fell in love with. When I met Tom (not his real name), I saw red flags. I had some concerns. I suggested to Pamela that she take her time, get to know Tom over several months before marrying him. Initially she agreed, however, a month later they married. Pamela became pregnant, she was in her midforties at the time. Tom was verbally abusive. About two years after the baby was born, Pamela decided to leave her husband and moved back to New York City. We lost touch. I did grieve losing our friendship, but Pamela needed to make a fresh start surrounded by her family. These are just two incidents of loss. We do go through the stages of grief with our losses. God is there, turn to Him, and tell Him of your sadness. He will comfort you. God bottles our tears. Psalm 56:8 (NLT) states, "You keep track of all my sorrows, You have collected all of my tears in your bottle. You have recorded each one in your book." God loves us so much that He keeps track of our sorrows and collects our tears. My bottle must be huge!

In 1988, I moved to Georgia to study for a master's degree in community counseling and a diploma in Christian counseling. I moved down before getting a job. I signed up for per diem (as needed) work at mental health hospitals and agencies. For several months, I worked and went to school not knowing what my schedule would be. I initially paid out-of-state tuition, rent, health insurance (COBRA), bills, and the car I owned would breakdown on average of once a month. Yet the Lord provided me with enough work to pay the bills. One morning, after working a night shift for an agency, I had been asleep for an hour when the telephone rang. The same agency had called saying they had a job for me three times per week and the company would work around my class schedule, and the money was very good. Even though I was very sleepy, I thought, "This sounds too good to be true." Then they explained the company was an abortion clinic. So here I am, needing to pay these bills every month with an unreliable car. Do I take the job and go against God according to the Bible? Or do I tell them no? I told them I would not take the job. When asked why, I stated, "Abortion is murder." I never received work from that agency again. However, several weeks later, one of the hospitals called stating they had a weekend position where I could work 7:00 p.m. to 7:00 a.m., Saturdays and Sundays, receive thirty-six hours of pay and health benefits. The Lord provides! God, at times, puts us through tests, this was one of mine. For the sake of a secure income, do I take the job at the abortion clinic or hold fast to God and His principles? I chose God.

Later, while I taught eleventh grade English in El Salvador, I used this experience to explain to my students that we all go through tests and trials. We need to know why we stand for something or believe something, not because our parents say so or because our minister states it is so. We need to read the Scriptures for ourselves. Pray to our Lord to guide us. Hold fast to His teachings.

After obtaining my master's degree in community counseling, I stayed in Georgia a few more years. I looked for jobs to combine counseling and nursing, visiting other states, but what jobs I could find, the money was less.

In the field of mental health things were changing. The hospital I worked for cut back on staff. We previously had plenty of staff to take patients to the tennis court, pool, or on a walk; staff to interact with them. I had one patient state that since we could not spend the time with her like before, she wouldn't be back. When staff cuts occurred, the patients felt more frustration, some acting out physically. It was becoming dangerous to work in any of the mental health hospitals in the area. I expressed this to my mother who said, "Come home." Now a part of me felt like I failed in not finding another job, but another part felt relief. We don't always understand why things happen, but God does. Sometimes when we pray, God gives us a different answer than the one we think we need or want. But He will always provide for us and we need to follow His lead. I went home at Christmas with my cat, Nikki, by early February I started work at a nonprofit mental health hospital close by. My mother and I grew closer. Then in the year 1996, I flipped through the television channels and found the *700 Club*. They had just completed a medical mission with Operation Blessing and the next trip would be in March 1997 to the Philippines. The Lord said, "You are going." I filled out the forms, obtained a passport, and prepared for the trip—getting vaccines for yellow fever, hepatitis A, and medicine for malaria.

I went to the airport only to find that my flight had been cancelled, the next flight to Los Angeles was in four hours. I thought, "I went through all of this and maybe not be able to go. I should give up, go home." But then I thought, "No, Satan would love that, something good will happen if I go."

I finally found an airline staff member who was able to reach the leaders of the mission to explain that my flight would arrive later. Los Angeles airport is huge with different buildings. When I got off the flight from Washington D.C., two other ladies going on the trip met me and took me directly to the boarding area. I was the last to check-in and we soon took off. Wow, what a long flight. Twenty hours, then four hours by bus to reach Olongapo, which was where the USA previously had an army base.

Philippines - Jeepney - USA WWII Jeeps
converted into transportation.

Driving from Manila to Olongapo was definitely a culture shock. People living in shacks and even some using cardboard boxes for shelter. The Filipinos converted the army base into a beautiful tourist section. The hotel was wonderful with terrific buffets for breakfast and supper, the tree-ripened mango and pineapple were fantastic. Our leaders stated, "If this is your first mission trip, do not expect this food to be on future trips." Behind our hotel was a jungle. After supper we went out to look at the trees, there was movement, the world's largest bats were waking up to fly the night skies. It was fascinating to watch them.

Monkeys behind the hotel - Philippines

While at the airport in Manila, another nurse and I shared a luggage cart. She asked if this was my first mission trip. I said yes. The nurse stated, "It won't be your last."

I thought, "How does she know, we just arrived." But she was right. Here I was at thirty-nine years old, going on my first mission trip. We were in the Philippines for two weeks. Operation Blessing had two areas, one for surgeries and one for a clinic. We offered medical and dental clinics together. They had a pharmacy area. I thought, "Bet they put this psychiatric nurse there." Yep, they did, along with a nurse who worked in a nursing home from Wisconsin. I learned how to setup a pharmacy for future trips with different churches. We had many volunteers from the local churches helping us, including a pharmacist who came for a few days but stated her husband threatened to take the children and leave. She risked losing her children to serve God with us, that touched my heart. We prayed her husband would not take the children from her.

Carol and Leesa at Pharmacy in Philippines.

One night while sleeping, I felt the bed sway. I had just experienced my first earthquake. No damage was done in the area. The team drove back to Manila. We had several hours until our flight back to Los Angeles. We went to a huge store that had several floors. I'm a June baby and had always wanted something with a pearl, which is my birthstone. I found a beautiful strand of pearls for only fifty dollars. What a blessing. The Lord cares even about our little desires such as a pearl necklace. Operation Blessing ministered to thousands of people during those two weeks. Many received the Lord as their savior through local volunteers in the counseling area of the clinic.

Surrender Your Struggles to God

Bat coming in at sunrise - Philippines

A team of missionaries from El Salvador joined us for the two weeks. I became friends with several of the interpreters, dentists, and doctors. They invited me to come visit El Salvador. I thought they were just being nice, but one friend said, "No, we want you to come down."

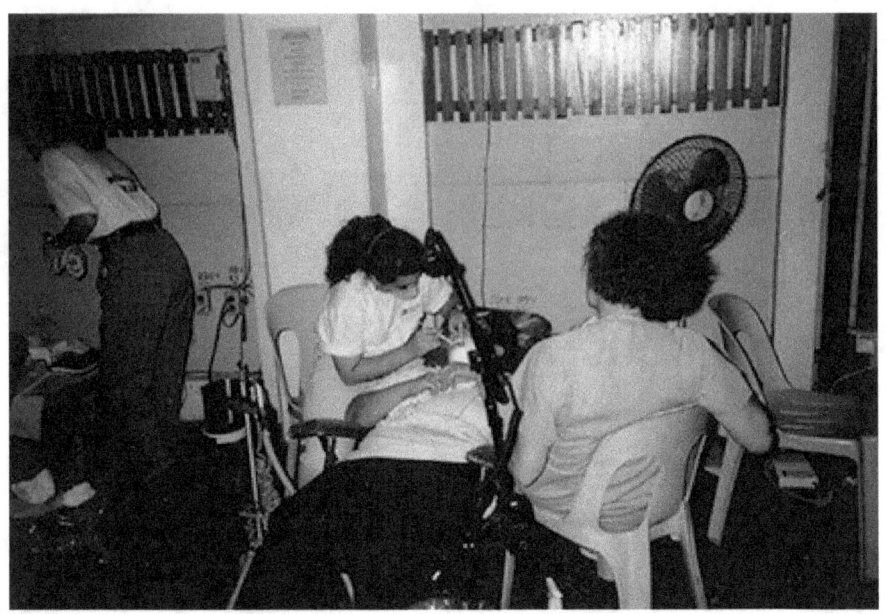

Dentist Veronica examining patient.

Surrender Your Struggles to God

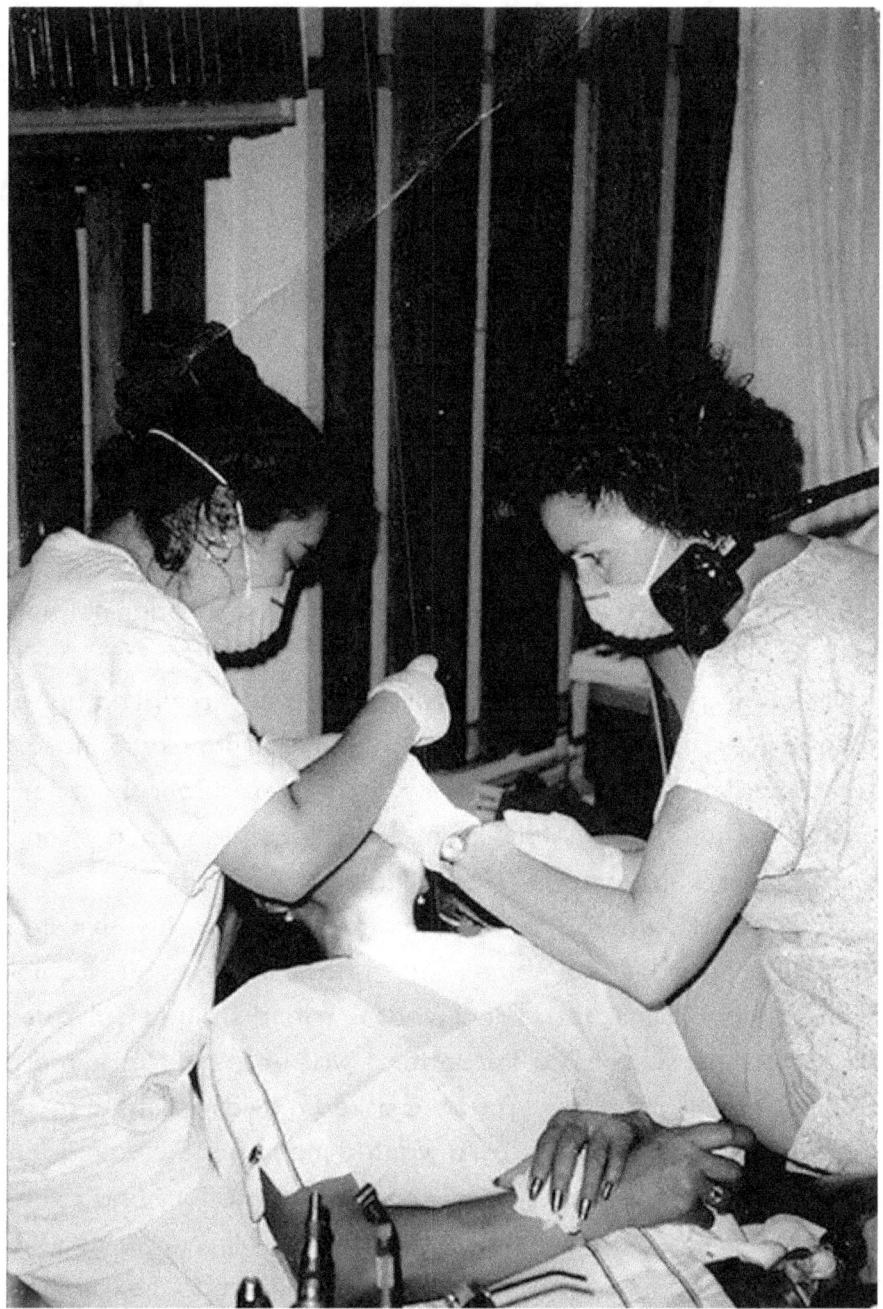

Philippines - El Salvadoran dentist Veronica examining patient.

In the fall of 1997, I took a vacation to San Salvador, El Salvador, where I saw a beautiful country that had many poor people. I helped out on a medical mission while there in the pharmacy. The dentists were in the next room. The lead nurse asked me to interpret, I said, "My Spanish is not good."

She said, "God will give you the ability."

And during that time, I did interpret between the staff from the States and the Salvadoran dentists. During this time, the Lord let me know I was coming back as a missionary. My friend, Sandra, with whom I stayed with, her father and son took me to their church, which was a large church with three Sunday services. They had a bilingual school and wanted Americans to come teach.

Over the next two years, I returned to El Salvador helping with medical clinics and visiting friends. During my first visit, while putting on my shoes for church, I heard a rumbling noise, followed by shaking. I asked if that was an earthquake. Sandra's father said yes, but just a little one. It registered four point nine on the Richter scale. A six point zero is considered a strong earthquake with damage to buildings.

The school wanted a recommendation from my minister. Pastor Paul (not his real name), sent a basic letter, but it was not encouraging for me to be received. A friend from El Salvador contacted me concerning this letter. I was upset, disappointed, and angry with my pastor. The Lord asked if I was willing to sever the relationship. I knew the Lord wanted me to go to El Salvador. I needed to confront the pastor. I hate confrontations and avoid them as much as possible. But I did approach him concerning the letter. Pastor Paul stated, "Teaching is not your work." I explained to him that there is much teaching in nursing; that teaching in a classroom setting would be different, but I could do it. Then

Pastor Paul said, "You don't have Bible class background." I reminded him of my diploma in Christian counseling and listed the courses I took. Then the pastor apologized to me, met with the board, and wrote a glowing report to the school. The church sent me monthly support while I taught at the school. I had to risk severing a relationship in order to follow what God wanted, and it turned out well. Pastor Paul and I are still in touch today.

El Salvador is a beautiful country in Central America, about the size of the state of Massachusetts. It is always warm. I lived in the capital city of San Salvador. My apartment was at the base of the San Salvador volcano. There are twenty-three volcanoes in El Salvador, six are considered active. One friend stated that Central America is nicknamed Hammock Land because of all the swaying from the earthquakes. There are two major seasons in El Salvador, dry and rainy. From November through April, it is warm and dry, no rain. November through February, trade winds blow, perfect time weather- wise to be in El Salvador. March and April in San Salvador feels like August up here, hot and humid. May through October it rains, sometimes only in the afternoons and evenings, sometimes all day. My challenge was when I washed my clothes and hung them out to dry, could I make it home from work to take down my clothes before it started to rain? Beans, rice, and corn are the main staples. The large meal of the day is lunch. Breakfast is beans and rice with sour cream, bread, and eggs. Supper is usually sandwiches, soup, beans, and rice or *pupusas*. *Pupusas* are tortillas made from corn or rice flour and stuffed with beans, or cheese, or pork, or *loroco* (a local herb). The *pupusas* are topped with a light tomato sauce and a pickled cabbage/carrot slaw. This you are to eat with your fingers. The first time I had *pupusas* was after church. My friends said, "You don't use a fork, use your fingers."

I replied, "Not this time, while I'm wearing a nice Sunday dress." But after that I learned to eat the *pupusas* with my fingers, tearing off a piece at a time.

I enjoyed the tropical fruits, especially mango. Other fruits were papaya, pineapple, cantaloupe, watermelon, oranges, lemons, limes, and of course, bananas and plantains. Buying mango back here in the States is not the same as getting tree-ripened mango from Central America (okay, you guys in south Florida, I know you have some too). Being only twelve degrees north of the equator, daylight usually lasts twelve to thirteen hours a day throughout the year. Sunrise just before 6:00 a.m. and sunset between 5:30 and 6:00 p.m. The sun was always up when I woke, having those nice rays coming in my window. The orchids are beautiful. The palm trees and other tropical trees and plants are numerous even in the capital city. I saw different birds.

Once a four foot iguana walked by our class window. The boys made jokes about making iguana burgers. I learned to check my shoes before putting them on, at least twice I found a scorpion in my shoe. When I moved to El Salvador, the country was eight years in recovery from a civil war that lasted from 1980–1992. Many doctors and dentists worked two jobs. They do not make the amount of money our doctors do in the States. I had friends who had their own clinic, then taught at the university. My personal dentist was a missionary from Colorado who married a Salvadoran and attended school in El Salvador to become a dentist. He also taught at the same school I did. If doctors and dentists need to work two jobs to buy food for their families and pay bills, think of all the other six million people in the country. If a middle-aged person loses his job, it is very difficult to find a new one. Businesses prefer to hire younger people. The median age in El Salvador is twenty-six (per El Salvador Demographics Profile 2017). As a result of poverty, some people steal, kidnap, or take part in gangs like MS-13.

One afternoon, while I taught English as a second language at the British school for some of the Spanish teachers, a teacher participating in the class stated that a boy in his son's class was kidnapped the day before. He asked for prayer. We prayed that God would help the boy be rescued or to escape. We found out later, that on the afternoon we prayed, there was only one person in the hotel room where they were holding the child hostage. The person fell asleep and the boy ran out of the room, found a housekeeper who helped him contact the police and his parents. Praise be to God! San Salvador means holy Savior, El Salvador means the savior. In downtown San Salvador, there is a statue called Momumento al Divino Salvador del Mundo (Monument to the Divine Savior of the World). It is a statue of Jesus standing on top of the world. El Salvador also has an area of spectacular Mayan ruins, including a pyramid that you can walk up the steps if you desire to.

Moving to El Salvador was definitely an adventure. The Lord had me there for several reasons, but a main one for me was learning dependence on Him. My parents taught me to be independent, don't trust others too much. So I always tried to solve things on my own. I knew we are to give the Lord our problems. I would say, "Here it is, Lord," then I would pick the problem back up. He had me in situations that I couldn't do anything about.

"Daughter, what can you do?" "Nothing."

"What can you do?"

"Depend on you to solve this." "Now you're getting it."

I had shipped my car down from Wilmington, Delaware, to San Pedro Sula, Honduras. I needed to pick up my car. Originally, a young friend from the States who was studying at the university was to accompany me to Honduras, but something occurred that he could not go. However, my friend Sandra's family had made me a part of their family, I was the American sister. Her older brother, Ricardo, went with me. The Lord definitely arranged this. Rick and I took a bus to San Pedro Sula. We went to get my vehicle. Rick spoke with them. The people were trying to have me pay more money. He was firm and told them it was all paid for. I owed nothing. After obtaining my car, which I had stuffed with a small TV, crockpot, microwave, dishes, and books, we drove back to El Salvador. Driving the frontier between the countries can be dangerous. Some people signal each other with flags to try to get someone to stop especially with USA plates or with possessions. An attempt was made to have us stop. An old man tried to run into our car from the other side of the road, but we were able to avoid being stopped. When serving God, He provides protection, perhaps His angels were surrounding the car. We arrived safely back in El Salvador. The lady I was staying with until the school found an apartment for me, asked what happened. The old man had managed to somehow take off my side-view mirror. She had Pastor Hector, who was headmaster of the school, come by. Pastor Hector explained, "Sister, you are in a dangerous country." God's intervention saved me. Once I had my car in El Salvador, it took several months to get a Salvadoran license plate and driver's license, so I still had my USA plates. The police setup road blocks using the orange construction cones. I got pulled over on average of once a week. The cops would ask, "Why are you here? You are taking a job away from a Salvadoran." Once, they even threatened to take my car. It took me awhile to realize some of the police wanted money. Finally, one day, I replied, "*Soy una missionera* (I am a missionary)." You could see it in their eyes—missionary means no money. After that, I would explain right away that I was a missionary and drove on. To get my driver's license and plates, I first needed an inspection, which per the mechanic, any vehicle over two years old did not pass; so I paid him some money, went to a different garage for a minor adjustment, more money, and returned to the inspection place and passed, again more money. El Salvador has the same basic driving rules as the USA, so they gave me a license without taking a test. I did need blood work done. They test for HIV and your blood type. I did like their driver's license, it contained my blood type (A+) and my medical allergies (penicillin and sulfa). It also listed my medications (synthroid and hypertension medicines). If an accident occurred and you couldn't communicate, the information was right there. "She needs blood, oh she's A+, start it right away." "Don't give penicillin, she's allergic." Personally, I think the USA could learn from El Salvador and incorporate at least the blood type and medication allergies on people's driver's licenses.

Shortly after moving into my apartment, a vigilante came by my door. I needed to pay ten dollars a month for protection. I explained I was new to the country, and wanted to talk to friends first before saying yes. That night I heard noises around my apartment. The next day, I paid the vigilante fee. During my two years there, no one tried to harm me or break into my apartment.

I taught third grade the first year and had the same students for fourth grade the next year per parents' requests. The students had classes in English through lunch, then another teacher would instruct the students in their Spanish curriculum. I enjoyed teaching the children who also taught me Spanish words and culture.

My third grade class was comprised of twenty-four students—twelve boys and twelve girls. Working with twenty-four different personalities is a challenge. A struggle I had within myself was encouraging some of the students to study. Math was a hard subject. The students did well with addition and subtraction, but memorizing multiplication tables was another matter. Several of the students refused in their own way to do so. No matter that I explained they would have trouble in Math in the future if they did not memorize their tables. People make choices, sometimes to their detriment, but we can encourage them and pray for them. I had one child, the youngest in the class, who would not do his homework or pay attention in class. He loved to doodle. Pedro definitely had artistic ability, no matter how much encouragement, he did not focus in class. Finally in May, Pedro came to me and stated, "I want to pass." I explained it was too late, he was failing in several subjects, both Spanish and English. The next year, Pedro repeated the third grade and did well, but it was difficult to see what Pedro was doing to himself. Some of the other children also had problems in the fourth grade when we started learning division. If you don't know your multiplication tables, you will have major difficulty with division. Most of the students finally did memorize their tables, but one did not and failed Math. Another student had a tendency to just write any number on his quizzes and was close to failing. After the third quarter, I explained to Armando that he was in danger of failing. Amazingly, the next test Armando scored a ninety-five! He could do the work, he knew his tables, just wanted to play. I believe parents struggle more intensely within themselves concerning their children. You teach, guide, set boundaries, but at times you watch your child make unwise decisions. We want to prevent the consequences from happening after making poor choices, but sometimes we must go through these consequences in order to learn. But the child still feels the results of the consequences, whether it is failing a grade or getting involved in a sexual relationship in their teen years. Studies show the area of reasoning in the brain does not mature until a person is in their midtwenties. A young person may have a credit card and buy several expensive items, then finding it difficult to pay off the credit card. As parents and other adults in their lives, aunts, uncles, teachers, we can pray for our students and give support and guidance. Proverbs 22:6 (NASB) states, "Train up a child in the way he should go. Even when he is old he will not depart from it."

As adults we need to realize that a child's feelings, concerns, and fears are real and important to them, even if we think it's not a serious matter, it is to the child. An example of this is a story about an eleven- year-old patient I'll call Malik. One morning while the students were getting ready for school a staff member I'll call Jason, called me back to Malik's room. I knocked on the door and entered. Malik had on his jeans and sneakers, but no shirt. He looked upset. When I asked Malik what was wrong, Jason said "Malik is upset with his chest." Malik had gynecomastia - breast tissue that forms due to hormonal changes in puberty. I explained to Malik that his chest was getting ready to grow, but before his chest could grow his body needed to make more skin and muscle for his chest to grow into. I also explained that this process would continue for about four years. Jason was an athletically built young man in his mid-twenties who was kind and caring with our patients. The students admired him. I told Malik that one day he would look like Mr. Jason. Malik's eyes got big and he turned to Jason. Jason explained that he went through the same experience when he was Malik's age. Malik felt relief and hope. When the day arrived for Malik to go home with his grandmother, he thanked us for helping him.

One student who attended my class in the third grade had some challenges. Carolina was new to the school. She did not start out in kindergarten with the rest of the students and wasn't accepted readily as part of the group at first. Also, Carolina struggled with English grammar and spelling. I tried different approaches with her and prayed. One day, during class, everything came together for her, Carolina understood! Praise God! Her grades improved. At the end of the year, Carolina and another student needed to take a makeup test to pass the year, but both did pass! Carolina's family moved to the States for the next year, I did miss her.

Miguel was an intelligent and kind boy. But at one point, during the third grade, Miguel was not completing assignments. I wondered what was going on. Finally, another teacher who was a family friend, told me Miguel's father had died when he was younger and his mother was currently in the hospital. One day, Miguel came in upset. He realized he did not make a project for science class of the solar system. I explained that his project could be to draw the solar system. He smiled, felt relief, and not only drew the planets in their orbits, but the asteroid belt between Mars and Jupiter too. Miguel received an A for his project. If you are a parent reading this, please inform your child's teacher of any major changes happening in your family situation so that the teaching staff can help your child work with his feelings and continue focusing in class. Teaching is a team effort between family and the school staff.

Before the fourth quarter, the English director asked me to take over the eleventh grade English class in the afternoon as that teacher was being dismissed. The first day I walked into the class, the students sang "American woman stay away from me."

I replied, "Nice try, but you can't get rid of me that easily." I didn't experience any problems with the students and taught the eleventh grade class the following year.

Hispanic families are very close. When my elementary students had a project to do, such as the solar system, every mother would arrive at the school at recess time with their children's projects and would be supportive of their children. They would also discipline their children. I had one child who refused to take a math test one day. Jose crumpled up the test and threw it away. He was given a score of zero. The next day his mother came in and asked if her son could retake the test. When I explained what transpired, she pulled Jose from the desk and took him outside. I don't know what happened, but the boy was contrite when he returned to class.

Social studies in the fourth grade was about all of the States. I talked with the students about Thanksgiving. I requested from the school if we could celebrate Thanksgiving. They agreed. The mothers were excited about celebrating Thanksgiving and asked what food to bring. I stated, "*Typicos* will be fine." *Typicos* would be beans and rice, *pupusas, tamales* (corn baked in husks or chicken and corn baked in banana leaves), and fruit.

They stated, "Oh no, we want American." The mothers made turkey with a tomato sauce, mashed potatoes, bread, and fruit.

I explained a tradition many families have, is to go around the table and state what we are thankful for, perhaps a new baby in the family, or maybe the father has a new job. Every child stood up and stated they were thankful for their families and for their teacher. Every adult was touched by the children's statements.

January of 2001 was interesting. The country of El Salvador changed the monetary base from the colon to the US dollar. Many people struggled with this. One afternoon, when I got home, I saw a lady selling *tamales* up and down the street. I went to buy some, but when she saw I had a dollar, she refused to sell, thinking I may cheat her. My students would ask me how many *colones* were in a quarter so they could buy some candy at recess. Some of the students had difficulty learning about the money differences, but the uneducated even more so. El Salvador used both currencies for a year, then went to the dollar only. Saturday, January 13, I was teaching at a language school for extra money. I normally had eight students in the class, but that day only three came. We felt a quake and I thought it was over, when suddenly the floor felt like sea waves, the light fixture came down. I shouted at my students to get outside. El Salvador just had a seven point six earthquake. Later, I found out that hundreds of people died. I took a friend home. First, we went to my apartment where the sliding glass door had jumped the track and was positioned precariously against the other door. We were able to put it back in place. I had a floor vase that broke and there was a crack in the garage wall. I scrambled us some eggs for our lunch, then drove to her house. She had several items broken, but no major damage. Two blocks from my apartment many families who lived in shacks lost their housing. The government provided tents for them to live in. The people were resilient. The children continued to play during the days after the earthquake, and the people would get together on Tuesday evenings worshipping and praising God. They lost their homes and yet they still praised God. I know the Lord says to give Him thanks, but I'm not sure if I could have praised Him directly after losing everything. I was definitely humbled by this experience. Schools closed until they could be examined by engineers.

The evening of the earthquake, I tried calling my mother. I was unable to get through. I sent my cousin, Brenda, an email asking her to call Mom. She emailed me back stating that she did contact Mom, but also that she rarely looks at her email on Saturday evenings, but something told her to. That was God. Sometimes computers can be a blessing. I also sent out an email to the churches who sent me support. The one pastor told me later that his daughter stated, "Dad, where is Leesa?"

"In El Salvador."

"They just had a major earthquake." They tried looking at the news for information, then finally checked the church email. I was safe. Praise God.

Exactly one month later, on Tuesday, February 13, we experienced a six point six earthquake. All of the girls stood around me in a circle until their parents arrived. The boys were a little further away, but I could see them. One of the boys would come over and say, "Miss Leesa, are you okay?"

"Yes, Mario, thank you."

This was the boys' way of knowing where I was, but I knew where they were.

When the schools closed, I volunteered at the Salvadoran Red Cross. We took care of the injured who came in. The Red Cross had our old brown oxygen tanks from the 1960s that we used on an ambulance driver having breathing difficulties. One of the patients was a man who cut his wrists. The doctor gave him a bar of soap, told him to wash up and leave. My American way of thinking, I was shocked. In the States we would have referred the man to a hospital for a psychiatric evaluation. There was a psychiatric hospital in the city, but the doctor sent him out. Another patient who was Salvadoran by birth but was a Canadian citizen, she had several cuts from the earthquake. She said her family moved to Canada after the last major earthquake fifteen years prior, and she returned for a visit when this earthquake struck. "I'm not coming back to El Salvador."

One of the nurses was a student doing her social year. When you attend the university, before you actually graduate and receive your diploma, you work a year for the country. If you're an engineer, you may be building bridges in a small mountain village for your social year. The staff did use sterile technique when helping the patients. The one thing that bothered me was they had a community towel for the staff that would be changed frequently, so I would dry my hands on a towel used by someone else. I prayed, "Lord, you have me here, I will trust that I will not get sick from someone else using this towel." I did not get sick, praise God!

After the two major earthquakes, El Salvador experienced many aftershocks for several months. One aftershock was a 5.7. It was shallow and felt like giant hands were pulling down my apartment building. No damage occurred, but I was scared. The epicenter was in San Salvador, not off the coast and I was alone in my apartment, not with my students. Most people experienced some symptoms of post-traumatic stress such as heightened reactions to the tremors, anxiety, irritability, insomnia and nightmares. Every time you felt a quake you'd wonder if this was going to be another big one. What would happen? Many people slept out on the streets afraid their houses would collapse. I slept in a T-shirt and shorts and kept my keys by the door for several months. I considered returning to the USA but remembered that I committed to teach for two years. God saw me through. I did go home for a month in the summer and returned to teach the second year.

One of the teachers at the school was married to a minister. They had a small church in the country. Beatrice requested I do some first aid teaching. An SUV or truck is a good thing to have in El Salvador, but a car may be another story. There were large bumps in some of the streets. I got to the church and instructed people in basic first aid. The church gave me ten dollars. As I drove back, I went over a large bump and lost my muffler. I went to a garage thinking a muffler would be expensive. They charged me eight dollars, so I still had two dollars from the church. God is good, He provides. One of the teachers at the language school requested I go to his wife's school where she was the principal to talk with the teachers about post-traumatic stress with their students. I visited five different schools. They had asked how to keep the students safe during an earthquake. I explained to do evacuation drills. If they know where to go, the students are less likely to panic. I found out later that one of the schools was doing a drill when the second earthquake struck.

I attended a small church where a dentist was the pastor. He had asked me to accompany him to two factories and talk with people there. This time I could talk about God and faith. I taught them some things to help their families such as vanilla and orange are comfort scents for children. They could put orange oil or vanilla on the pillows. I also explained that yes, we could die in the next earthquake, but we could be hit by a bus this afternoon (let me tell you, the busses owned the road, that was a real possibility of happening). Do you know Jesus? Have you asked Him into your life? One man received the Lord into his life. That was a first for me, to be used to give a message and have someone receive salvation, I was ecstatic.

I had friends who lived in central Pennsylvania in a rural area. They would go to different churches and sing. At a Wednesday evening service, a member of the church said to their pastor, "I heard there was a bad earthquake in El Salvador, what can we do?" My friends, Sam and Marsha, stated they had a missionary friend in El Salvador that they could send money to and the money would go directly to the people. The church sent over two hundred fifty dollars which was used to buy rice, beans, and powdered milk that we distributed to the poor. This was another way God uses people. The woman had a concern about the people of El Salvador, not knowing that the visiting singers had a friend who was a missionary there. The church helped to minister to the people in need by sending money and providing food. God is good.

The Presbyterian church I grew up in sent me support. They also were a blessing to a family of four students. The father was a pastor of a small church. He was having financial difficulty, and could not pay the tuition for the church school. For many people, having their children attend a school that taught English was a way to help their children attain better jobs, and go on to college upon graduation. My church sent enough money to cover the family's tuition for the rest of the year.

At the end of the school year, I came home to the States for a month. The first thing I wanted was a warm shower, my apartment did not have hot water. The buildings also did not have screens on the windows, but had jalousie windows that you crank open. To prevent being bitten by mosquitos at night,

I bought an oscillating fan that I set close to my bed. They had dengue fever in El Salvador. There are two types of dengue fever. The first is like having a bad case of flu, including your bones and muscles aching, headache, fever, swollen lymph nodes, exhaustion, and a rash. The second type of dengue fever is hemorrhagic; sudden fever, severe abdominal pain, bleeding under the skin and shock. Many people die from hemorrhagic dengue fever, especially young children. I had one student who contracted dengue fever, the flu type, she missed two weeks of school and was in the hospital. I went to her house to catch Elena up on her schoolwork. She was an excellent student.

I went home for Christmas and summer breaks. I brought back with me to El Salvador several large bottles of ibuprofen and Epsom salts.

A man in the small church had his leg in a cast and pain. He could not afford to buy medicine, so I gave him a bottle of ibuprofen and explained to him to take the pills with food. Also, there was a young man on my street who dearly loved his mother. From time to time he would ask for rice or beans which I would give him. Then his mother had pain. I never met her, but sent over a baggie with ibuprofen. This happened several times. One day, the young man came by and stated they were selling mangoes (I love fresh mango), so I gave him two dollars. He brought me over a huge trash bag filled with mangoes, no way I could eat all of those. I took the mangoes to school where the cafeteria ladies made use of them. I believe the huge bag of mangoes was the woman's way to repay me for the medicine. The Epsom salts I had planned to have my students make crystals with dye. However, a mother of one of my students stated her son (brother to my student) hurt his arm. What could be done to help? He had been seen by a doctor. I went home at lunch and brought back the Epsom salts, and explained for the mother to have her son soak his arm for twenty minutes. The mother returned the following week and said the Epsom salts had really helped in the healing. Again, God's hand in action.

People state we remember where we were on September 11, 2001. My apartment had cable so I would receive news from the States. I listened to CNN while getting ready for work. I turned off the TV and drove to work. At recess, another teacher said, "Isn't it sad about the plane crash?"

"What crash?"

"A plane flew into the twin towers in New York City."

I thought, "How sad, a single engine plane crashed into a building." My friend said, "No, it was a big plane. Then another one hit the Pentagon."

When I heard that, I became very concerned. I had left my apartment three minutes before the first plane flew into the twin towers. I asked the English director if I could miss the English meeting at lunch today and check out the news. The school sent me a substitute teacher and let me go early. One of the TV stations stated that Camp David was on the terrorist list. I have family that live several miles from there. I called my mother, everyone was fine. Her concern was me, but we are not being attacked here. I was truly thankful that everyone was safe. September 15 is Independence Day for most of Central America (El Salvador, Guatemala, Honduras, Nicaragua, and Costa Rica). Instead of celebrating their Independence Day, the Salvadoran government cancelled all festivities in honor of the mourning the USA was going through. This action by a third world country touched my heart, giving up their own celebrations to commiserate with us. There are numerous nations who care about the USA and pray for us.

At recess, the boys usually play soccer (futbol), the girls talked or had quiet games, sometimes asking to play with my hair. One day, a boy in the other fourth-grade class brought in a plastic bat and ball. He and a friend were trying to hit the ball, but no luck. I went over to the two boys. I showed the boy with the bat how to stand, how to swing the bat. The first pitch, he hit the ball! Immediately all the boys and a few of the girls came running over and lined up. They wanted to learn also. The students were watching even though they were engaged in other activities. This incident taught me that no matter what we do, we are being observed. People watch us, see what we do, how do we react. As a Christian, what am I showing today? Am I showing Christ's love? Or am I giving in to feelings of anger, fatigue, or frustration? If I am tired, do I show perseverance? What do they see? Do people who observe you want what you have, which is the love of Christ?

God uses everyday situations and objects to have us help others, like the boy with the injured arm. The Epsom salts helped in the healing. Stopping to talk with someone, give some encouragement. We do not know what people may be experiencing. Perhaps they are in despair, depressed, considering suicide. God can use you without you even being aware that you changed something in a positive way for someone. At times we may get a thought about someone we care for. A nurse I worked with in Georgia had considered suicide from time to time. One day, while I was seven hundred miles away from Georgia, I received an urgent thought, "Call Julie, call Julie right now." I called her. Julie was planning to commit suicide that night. After talking with her, she contacted her therapist and received help. We never know how we may be used to help others.

During my time in El Salvador, I had another challenge. I took a course in ministerial studies at the Univerisidad Evangelica. The course was ten months, one class per month for four hours on Saturday mornings. Most of the classes had a book to be read and a report written; most of the information I had previously in my counseling classes, but the challenge was taking it in Spanish. I did not have any English speaking friends to depend on, but going through these classes, my Spanish comprehension improved, and this *gringa* even managed to be second in the class of twenty some students. First place was Juanita who was the pastor's fiancée. She corrected my grammar when I wrote my reports. My most challenging moment at the university was giving a five-minute sermon. We were each given a verse and had to write a short sermon on. Some people in the class were called to get up and give their speech including me. My verse had to deal with coveting, so I made it fun with coveting a lot of shoes, or someone having an expensive car. I was nervous and gestured with my hands a lot. My speech teacher in college would have marked me down for all of that, but my professor praised my animation—different culture. I thought I was really going to be criticized especially for my Spanish grammar. I can communicate, but my grammar has much to be desired. Instead, the professor gave me support.

There was a woman in my neighborhood who cleaned houses. She came over on Friday afternoons to clean my apartment. Her pay was six dollars (normal rate was three dollars, but I wanted to give her more). One of her children came with her and he watered the plants on the patio and helped with the trash. I gave him one dollar. After that she made sure that one of her children accompanied her. She was surprised in December when

I told her I would be going to the States for three weeks that I paid her for. "But I'm not working."

"No, but it is because I'm going away and you are being paid, plus a little more for Christmas."

When it was time for me to return to the States after teaching for two years, I gave her my plates, silverware, sheets, towels, pots, and pans. But what she asked for were the clothespins. This woman couldn't afford a dollar for a pack of clothespins, of course I gave them to her. She also took out of my wastebasket the makeup I discarded. Some of the teachers came over to buy items—microwave, TV, crockpot, fan. Having the apartment empty, besides my luggage, felt surreal. I only had sandwich fixings in the refrigerator. I left the next morning.

After the second year of teaching at the school, I returned to the States. The first time I drove, I saw the orange cones and immediately got out my passport and license, then I realized the cones were for construction, not the police. Another thing to readjust to was all the different brands of food in the supermarket. How many soups are there? Campbell's, Progresso, generic, fat free, low sodium, regular, many choices. Even with the readjustments, I was happy to be back home in the USA.

Upon returning, I started looking for a job. I searched for several weeks and went on interviews, when the Lord blessed me with a job I desired for years—school nurse at a school for the deaf and hearing impaired. I have enjoyed helping students and interacting with the staff for the past fifteen years. I'm also using my Spanish on occasion, talking with family members concerning medical needs.

Iquitos Peru - Plaza de Armas de la Ciudad.

I lived with my mother, saving money and finally put a down on a house. I have a beautiful mountain view from my front porch. I found a wonderful church with ministers who preach the word of God, wonderful worship, has a focus on missions and having fun. I've been on four mission trips with my church, one to a mountain town in Nicaragua where we helped build a school, and three to Iquitos, Peru. You can't drive to Iquitos, only arrive by plane or boat. Planes only fly in the morning and evening due to the heat and steam from the jungle. Iquitos sits on the Amazon River. We had two teams in Peru, one to help build a church, and also a medical team. While on these trips, my position was intake. I had local volunteers ask for the chief complaints the clients had, and then I spoke with them, and wrote the problems and symptoms in English for our doctors who had local interpreters. In a week we saw about a thousand people. The people are poor and can't afford to go to a clinic or pharmacy to pick up medicine.

Surrender Your Struggles to God

Nicaragua - Building Church School.

Leesa King

Nicaragua - Building a Church School - Our helpers.

Surrender Your Struggles to God

Leesa listening to girl's lungs.

Cheryl Kenny CRNP helps a patient.

On one trip, I was developing an ear infection. One of the doctors came with me to the pharmacy. "Oh, that medicine is very expensive, one hundred and twenty dollars in the States." She was so surprised that the same medicine in Peru was ten dollars, still a lot of money for the people in the area. The mode of transportation in Iquitos is motor taxi. It looks like a three-wheeled motorcycle with a buggy on top. Being on a dirt road was scary, especially when they would race each other. One of the motor taxis I was in tipped over, no injuries besides some sore muscles. The missionary was surprised I went to the clinic the next day. She said that happened to another team, and the lady stayed in her room for the rest of the week. But since I wasn't hurt, I wanted to continue to serve.

Surrender Your Struggles to God

Motor taxi.

Motor taxi in Iquitos.

On another trip, my roommate needed to return to our room, so I was alone in the motor taxi. We had several motor taxis leaving the hotel at the same time to go to the clinic site. The driver took me in another direction. I got out and started walking. I prayed for the Lord to help me. He sent two boys about the age of eleven to twelve who spoke English. We found another motor taxi that I asked to take me back to the hotel, the boys came with me. The local missionary was waiting for me there. The Lord protected me and sent help. The next day, one of the motor taxis tried to take two women in their twenties away, however, a man in our group who was originally from Costa Rica saw what was happening and told his driver to follow them. They were able to stop the vehicle and returned to the clinic site. The thief comes only to steal and kill and destroy; I came that they may have life, and have *it* abundantly." (John 10:10 NASB). "Pray without ceasing" (1Thess 5:17 NASB).

Seeing the Amazon was incredible. Iquitos is an inland port. The Amazon is already a few miles across and much more to go through in Brazil. Iquitos was a part of the rubber baron period. People came to Iquitos for the latex of rubber trees to create tires for bicycles back in the late 1880s. There are several different native tribes in the Amazon region surrounding Iquitos. We got to meet the Boras. A family unit would walk an hour from their lodgings and meet with tourists. They would talk about their life, did some dances including the Anaconda dance where they would have the tourists join in. Afterward, they sold some products—blowguns, seed necklaces, baby anaconda spine necklaces (my nieces loved those), and purses made from tree bark. We had an afternoon of canoeing, we saw houses on stilts in the rivers just like you see in National Geographic. The children were playing ball in the water (and the water really does spin the opposite way below the equator). I saw a little girl around the age of seven washing her clothes in the river. On another afternoon, we took a large banana boat with a thatched roof and went out on the Amazon and its tributaries. At times it rains so much the trees are covered. We were in the treetops. We saw pink river dolphins, caimans, turtles, and piranha (they do have teeth). We stopped to visit an animal sanctuary seeing a beautiful jaguar and monkeys. We were told to hold on to our eyeglasses because the monkeys liked to snatch them away. The hotel we stayed at had good food. Breakfast they served eggs, bread, juices—pineapple, papaya, and orange. Also fresh fruit, mini bananas (these are sweet bananas) and fresh papaya. Supper was meat and potatoes, sometimes lentils; but for dessert, they always served Jell- O, because Americans love Jell-O.

River tributary to Amazon - Going through treetops.

Boy collecting on river tributary to Amazon.

Surrender Your Struggles to God

House on stilts.

Girl washing clothes in river.

Missionary Steve interprets for Bora tribe.

While on the trips, watch what you eat. Do not eat raw vegetables. Cooked vegetables, yes. On one trip to Peru, we flew back to Lima and had time to shop and eat lunch before our flight back to Miami. There was a restaurant from the Southwestern United States that I had eaten at in El Salvador, so I thought it was safe. I ordered a chicken ceasar salad. That was a mistake. After getting home, I had bad diarrhea, going to the bathroom frequently. I had gone to work when my supervisor realized how often I was using the bathroom, she sent me home. I took loperamide (Imodium) which didn't work. I called the doctor who said to take bismuth (Pepto-Bismol). That worked. Also, drink bottled water. Do not ask for ice for your drinks as the ice is probably made with local water. When brushing your teeth, you want to use bottled water not tap in case you swallow some.

Lima Cathedral.

There was a desk clerk at the hotel during the evenings who was taking English classes. I enjoyed helping him with his lessons. One I remember was the differences with there, their, and they're; three words that sound the same but with different meanings.

The last trip to Iquitos, the medical team went to a remote Indian village. All of the local interpreters went, so I became the interpreter for the construction team. It was fascinating watching them put up a tin roof. We did not have enough tin sheeting, so I asked a local if they knew where a hardware store was. He and the construction crew leader went in a motor taxi to obtain more tin sheeting. The team finished the job just as a storm broke. The sound of the rain hitting the tin roof was calming. Also, that day, I looked out the window and saw a green parrot in a tree, its natural habitat.

On one of the trips to Peru, I gave a talk to all of the missionaries. I explained that they are serving God by being here, but that Satan does not like it and will try to attack. The attacks may be in ways that you do not expect. You may feel depressed after returning. When I went to the Philippines, we found out several weeks later that they had a bad monsoon period, major flooding. You'd think, "What did we accomplish?" But then you remember, yes, we did touch people's lives. Yes, some asked Jesus into their hearts, and local churches invited them to attend. If you feel you are being led by the Lord to serve in missions, either short-term or long-term, please keep this in mind.

> For our struggle is not against flesh and blood, but against the rulers, against the powers, against the world forces of this darkness, against the spiritual forces of wickedness in the heavenly places. (Eph. 6:12, NASB)

Have fellowship with other believers, pray together. Put on your armor of God.

> Therefore, take up the full armor of God, so that you will be able to resist in the evil day, and having done everything, to stand firm. Stand firm therefore, having girded your loins with truth, and having put on the breastplate of righteousness, and having shod your feet with the preparation of the gospel of peace; in addition to all, taking up the shield of faith with which you will be able to extinguish all the flaming arrows of the evil one. And take the helmet of salvation, and the sword of the Spirit which is the Word of God. (Eph. 6:13-17, NASB)

Keep praying, reading your Bible, being obedient to His word. You are a warrior for the kingdom of God.

While studying in college, I attended praise and prayer meetings on Wednesday evenings. I would silently agree with the people who prayed aloud. I didn't like public speaking. One evening, the pastor said, "Only a handful of people are saying the prayers. I will assign each person a prayer topic." I was to pray for Joe who was sick. I rehearsed in my mind over and over until it was my turn to pray. After doing this for a while, I realized that I don't need to say anything special. Jesus is our friend and He is with us. I needed to pray like He is sitting with me, whatever is on my heart, and if it is just one short sentence, then that's enough. Since then I've prayed with people stating my concerns for them and others. Prayer is talking to God. Let Him know how you feel even if you are angry with Him. Yes, He already knows, but God wants to hear from you. Our Lord desires for us to develop a close relationship with Him. Thank Him for everything, even the little things. "Oh, I misplaced my keys, help me, Lord. Oh, there they are, thanks, Lord." You may want to say good morning to Him as you drive to work. Keep praying, conversing with our Lord.

For our high school yearbook, they asked what your plans were. Mine was to become a nurse and then get married. The first occurred, I am a nurse. However, the second did not. Throughout my years, I rarely dated. I wondered what was wrong with me. Am I too tall? Self-esteem issues would pop up concerning this. People would say, "Oh, your man will come along when you least expect him to." Well, I'm sixty years old now, and it hasn't happened. Sometimes the Lord says no. I look back and wonder. I am a loyal person. I think if I married, maybe I would have put my husband first in my life instead of God. Whatever the reason, I never married. But I have done missions, seen other countries, and obtained a master's degree which may never have happened if I was married. The Lord knows I love children. I'm a school nurse and was a teacher in El Salvador. God has allowed children in my life, just not in the typical way through marriage. Do I feel lonely at times? Yes, but we are never alone because God is always with us. Marriage is not the ultimate state of social happiness. Many marriages end in divorce. If both people are not serving the Lord together, there will be problems. Perhaps God has spared me from some difficult times that may have emotionally torn me apart. If you are reading this, think through your life. Yes, having a companion is good, but we have all we need in our Lord. He is Jehovah Jireh, our provider.

One of my personality traits is worry. I worry about what might happen, try to figure out what to say or do before things happen. Many times they never materialize or have a different outcome than what I anticipated. Looking back on my life now, I see that if God allowed me to become a parent, I would have been a greater worrier not warrior. As it is, I have a tendency to perseverate in saying some prayers over and over again throughout the day if something is on my mind. I try to remind myself of Philippians 4:6 (NLT), "Don't worry about anything; instead pray about everything." Tell God what you need, and thank Him for all he has done. 1 Peter 5:7 (NLT) states, "Give all your worries and cares to God, for He cares about you."

Coping skills are ways to help ourselves reduce stress and anxiety. Some people enjoy journaling, writing your feelings in a journal and reading them later, finding out what some of the triggers are for yourself. Some people enjoy walking, or working out at the gym to release some frustration. Others listen to music, have a CD of hymns, worship music, or classical music. Some people enjoy coloring in the intricate design coloring books. Knitting helps others. Reciting favorite Bible passages. If you are in a stressful situation, perhaps you can take a time out, step away, take some deep breaths, or go through your body starting with your feet, tightening them for a few seconds then release the muscles and move up to your legs. This technique helps the body to relax. If work is stressful, you may want to give yourself thirty to sixty minutes when you come home to do some activity. Maybe have a quiet place where you keep your CD player, coloring materials, needles and yarn, or other activities you enjoy such as a puzzle book. Allow yourself this time, you are worth it. Stress may lead to a depletion of a brain chemical called serotonin. There is a class of antidepressants that help with serotonin if needed. Foods that contain tryptophan may help also. Tryptophan is a precursor to serotonin. Some foods that contain tryptophan are turkey, chicken, beef, whole grains, nuts, seeds, cheese, eggs, and dark chocolate. Have a plate of spaghetti with meatballs or macaroni and cheese (using whole grain pasta products of course).

We are human. We have many insecurities throughout our lives. One thing is for sure, God loves us and sent Jesus to live among us, lead a perfect life, and died on the cross for us so that we may spend eternity with Him. Our Lord desires us to have a relationship with Him. Larry Crabb wrote about the PAPA prayer:

> P — present yourself to God without pretense. Be a real person in the relationship. Tell Him whatever is going on inside of you that you can identify.
> A — attend to how you are thinking of God. Again, no pretending. Ask yourself, "How am I experiencing God right now?" Is He a vending

machine, a frowning father, a distant, cold force? Or is He your glorious strong but intimate Papa?

P — purge yourself of anything blocking your relationship with God. Put into words whatever makes you uncomfortable or embarrassed when you're real in your relationship with Him. How are you thinking more about yourself and your satisfaction than about anyone else, including God and His pleasure?

A — approach God as the "first thing" in your life, as your most valuable treasure, the person you most want to know. Admit that other people and things really do matter more to you right now, but you long to want God so much that every other good thing in your life becomes a "second thing" desire.

The PAPA prayer is the best way I've discovered to develop and nourish the relationship with God given to me by Jesus through His life, death, and resurrection. Relational prayer provides the Spirit with a wide-open opportunity to do what He loves most to do, to draw me into the heart and life of the Father and make more like the Son (article in Conversations Journal Fall 2006).

The PAPA prayer may take time. You need a quiet time, a quiet area to look at yourself, your feelings, fears, and needs. I know I need to practice this much more than what I do. Quick prayers are wonderful, but looking within ourselves, taking our time to come into His presence brings us closer to God. He desires for us to know Him more. Prayer time is not just a time of telling God what we want or need. It is also a time of acknowledging who He is, what He has done for us. Giving thanks for His love, grace, mercy, protection, and provisions. We take so much for granted. Many times going through crises brings us closer to God. Develop your relationship more. Read your Bible, and pray.

Forgiveness is a process. Depending on the type of hurt, disappointment, or broken trust you have experienced, the amount of time for healing will vary. Many people say forgive and forget. We as humans do not forget, the memory may be buried deep until we experience something that reminds us of a previous situation, perhaps something in childhood. Whatever it is, we do need to forgive. When we do not forgive, several things may occur. You may develop physical problems such as hypertension. You may have anger stay with you. Once during my student nurse days, I had a patient in the mental health unit who went in and out from the hospital for ten years because he could not forgive a girlfriend who broke up with him. This man was so consumed by anger and hurt that he could not work. While studying for my master's degree, I worked with an aide who was also going through the counseling program. Emily (not her real name) was from a western state. Her father sexually abuse her. When she turned eighteen, Emily decided to move to Georgia to attend college. Emily put distance between herself and her abusive father. Sometimes this is what we need to do. Do we need to be around the person who gave us pain? Forgiveness does not mean you have to share personal concerns with them. If you have to work with the person, be courteous and professional without getting personal. If you don't need to be around the person who caused the pain, you may want to step back and assess your relationship. Do you want to continue with the relationship/friendship? Can you approach this person and discuss the problem? Is there a misunderstanding? Do you need time away before talking with them? Take the time you need to examine your feelings and pray. Sometimes due to our past experiences, we may perceive something in a different manner than what the person intended. But sometimes you need to let a relationship go. People can be in our lives for a short time or a long time. But we all affect each other. Seek out our Lord, let Him know how you are feeling. When you need to forgive and you find it difficult to do, cry out to God. Talk to Him, tell Him how you feel even if you are angry with God, let Him know that because He already knows! Give God your situation and state, "I forgive _____." Then when the situation comes to mind, remind yourself that you have already given the situation to our Lord and have forgiven the person. You will find that the pain will become less until the day you remember the situation and no longer feel the pain or anger. Your healing has occurred! Families experience emotional pain at times. As children we may sense tension in the house, but not realize that a parent is ill, or that there are financial struggles or relationship issues. Sometimes parents take their frustrations out on their children. If you have memories of criticism, anger, or hurt from family members; talk with our Lord, forgive your family. You may want to talk with family members now that you are older and start healing your relationships. About thirty years ago I discussed some issues with my mother. Afterwards our relationship became closer.

    I have been getting mammograms on a regular basis, at the age of fifty, my insurance plan allowed one per year. When I went for a mammogram at the age of fifty-six, they found a lump. I saw a breast surgeon who stated there was a fifty-fifty chance of it being cancer. I underwent a lumpectomy, CANCER, and more than what they thought; so another surgery to remove more tissue.

My next appointment with the surgeon, he told me that I needed a mastectomy. I felt scared. I would be losing a part of me, a part that identified my femininity. You do grieve when you lose a body part, even when it is necessary to save your life. You may be asking, "Didn't you feel the lump on self-breast exams?" No, I didn't feel it and neither did the surgeon. It was deep in the tissue. One of the other nurses I worked with came with me to my first appointment with an oncologist. She wrote down everything. I was very grateful to Donna for accompanying me and writing what the doctor stated, because when faced with the knowledge that you have cancer, you forget half of what the oncologist says. I had a PET scan before I was scheduled for a mastectomy. PET scan is positron emission tomography. They give you a radioactive drink then put you through a machine that detects changes at the cellular level. Amazing what we can do in medicine today. Depending on what was found would determine if I had chemotherapy first or the mastectomy. My PET scan was scheduled on March 17. The mastectomy was scheduled for March 19. The eighteenth was a day of waiting and praying. The church secretary called to see how I was doing. While talking to the secretary, my cellphone rang. The oncologist was calling. She asked how I was doing. I replied, "You tell me." The PET scan showed the cancer had metastasized into the lymph nodes under my right arm, but nowhere else, praise God! Then I spoke with the secretary who said, "I heard, good news."

I underwent a third surgery in a month's time, a simple mastectomy, which meant they left the skin so I could get reconstruction of the right breast done in the future if I decided to. The surgeon prayed with me prior to the mastectomy. Upon awakening in the recovery room, my doctor stated he got it all. It did involve three lymph nodes, he removed ten. The doctor stated the cancer was an aggressive form. The oncologist stated I was in stage 3A. My oncologist stated I needed to see a radiation oncologist as I would need radiation treatments after receiving chemotherapy. Again, a nurse friend named JoAnn came with me to meet with the doctor.

The stages of breast cancer according to the American Cancer Society are as follows:

- Stage 0—cancer cells only found in a duct, not in surrounding tissue.
- Stage IA—tumor two centimeters or less, no lymph node involvement.
- Stage 1B—tumor two centimeters or less and has spread to one to three axillary (underarm) lymph nodes or in the mammary lymph nodes.
- Stage IIA—tumor two centimeters or less and has spread to one to three axillary lymph nodes with the cancer being larger that two millimeter in the lymph nodes or tiny amounts of cancer found in the internal mammary lymph nodes or the tumor is larger than two centimeters, less than five centimeters, but cancer hasn't spread to lymph nodes.
- Stage IIB—tumor larger than two centimeters, less than five centimeters, and has spread to one to three axillary nodes and/or tiny amounts found in mammary lymph nodes or tumor larger than five centimeters but has not gone into the axillary lymph nodes.

- Stage IIIA—tumor five centimeters or less spread to one to nine axillary lymph nodes or it has enlarged the internal mammary lymph nodes. Cancer has not spread to distant sites.
- Stage IIIB—tumor has grown into the chest wall or skin and one of these: (a) Not spread to lymph nodes, (b) spread to one to three axillary lymph nodes or found in internal mammary lymph nodes, (c) spread to four to nine axillary lymph nodes or has enlarged the internal lymph nodes.
- Stage IIIC—tumor any size, spread to ten or more axillary lymph nodes or may have spread to lymph nodes under or above the collarbone.
- Stage IV—tumor can be any size, but the cancer has spread to distant lymph nodes or organs.

My cancer tumor was 2.3 cm × 2.1 cm × 2.1 cm and in surrounding tissue plus three axillary nodes—stage III A.

After the mastectomy, I had a drainage tube for several weeks. Then waiting a few weeks before starting the chemotherapy. I was warned of the side effects. The chemotherapy was setup. I was to receive two types of chemotherapy, one day every two weeks for the first two months. Then a third type of chemo, one day a week for three months.

First thing to happen, I would lose my hair after the second session. JoAnn accompanied me to a shop that sold wigs and worked with cancer patients. She helped me pick out a wig, which was a challenge. I'm tall and have a large bone structure. My head size is on the high end of the normal range. I needed a large wig. What did they have? Mediums and smalls. It took a couple of hours going through catalogs before finding one I liked. After purchasing the wig, I found it too hot. I received the chemotherapy during the hot months of May to October. My mother sewed some large bandanas for me, which were much cooler and definitely easier to wash. After the second session, my scalp started to hurt. I ran my fingers through my hair and clumps would come out. JoAnn watched me do this and said, "Please stop!" A couple of days later, I went to the beautician and had my head shaved. This was definitely better than feeling my scalp ache. The beautician refused payment. Shaving my head was her gift to me. The next side effects were fatigue and nausea. They had given me an anti- nausea medicine to take after the chemo sessions. You may be wondering if I stopped working. No, I didn't. The doctor told me that I would feel worse the second to third days after receiving the chemotherapy, so I scheduled the chemo for Thursdays, worked Fridays, then stayed at home in bed for the weekends. Actually, after working every day, I went to bed. It seemed all I could do was go to work and then I was done. I've felt tired at times before especially working double shifts, but this was fatigue. Your body feels drained. It's hard to do things. If I didn't work, I would worry and just stay in bed. Work was therapeutic for me, as well as providing income. My friend, Cynthia at church wanted to make me something to eat, I said chicken with vegetables. She made me a chicken-rice-broccoli casserole, which I normally enjoy. Cynthia brought it to me at work and I thanked her. I took two bites and couldn't handle it. My stomach was not accepting the broccoli, I gave the casserole to my coworker.

When diagnosed with breast cancer, the hospital gave me a breast cancer goodie bag that contained a book about eating while receiving chemotherapy. Of course it stressed healthy foods, plenty of fruits, and vegetables, but for me, most of those foods I couldn't eat. I ate green beans, peas, carrots, and lettuce. Fruit—apples, grapes, peaches, strawberries, definitely no tropical fruits like bananas or oranges. Meat—usually chicken or turkey, but plain. I ate a lot of rice or noodles with chicken broth or cream of chicken soup. Scrambled eggs were the easiest to make, so I ate eggs for supper frequently. I couldn't eat anything spicy or cooked with onions or peppers. Salad dressing was limited to ranch or caesar. If I got together with friends, my go-to meal was always chicken caesar salad. Sometimes, even smelling certain spices or foods made me nauseous. I even stopped eating chocolate. Like most women, I enjoyed eating chocolate a couple times a week, but that changed with the chemotherapy. Today, I eat chocolate on occasion, but not like I used to which is a good thing. It was a year or longer, after the chemo was finished, that I could enjoy some of these foods again. Most of the time, I didn't go out in crowds. I stopped going to church, but listened to podcasts or pastors on the internet. I went to the grocery store on hours most people didn't.

    Throughout all of the chemotherapy and radiation treatments, I had the support of family and friends. One friend came and cleaned my house twice, she definitely earned jewels in her crown! Some people would call me, some sent cards. My cousin, Brenda, sent me a card after the second month of chemotherapy. The card showed a turtle walking. You could see his footprints of where he had come from and the path ahead yet to go. It was slow and, yes, I had a ways to go, but I got through the first round of chemotherapy. My cousin apologized for not contacting me sooner. I said, no, I needed that card at that time. God will send you pick-me-ups through friends, family, church members. A gift I received from a secretary at the school, the secretary's mother who never met me, and a teacher was an electronic reader. Someone who never met me helped to purchase the reader. Amazing! A family at church bought me a portable CD player so I could listen to worship music while receiving chemotherapy. If you have a loved one, friend or church member who is going through cancer or another long-term illness, please call them or send a card, it means so much. But the most important thing to do is pray. After I had finished with the chemo and radiation, and felt well enough to start attending church, I asked the pastor if I could say a little something. I thanked them for the cards, gifts, and food, but especially for the prayers. Many people say, "Oh, the only thing I can do is pray." I'm here to tell you, the most awesome and powerful thing you can do is pray. Prayer is bringing your concerns to God. I had a picture in my head of God hearing all those prayers and turning to Gabriel saying, "Hey, Gabriel, that's #4726!" People who have never met me were praying, friends would ask if their church or a relative's church could pray for me—absolutely! I don't turn down any prayers!

Another situation to work with while undergoing treatments is to avoid crowds, not to get sick. Prior to starting chemotherapy, my nurse practitioner administered a tetanus booster and pneumonia vaccine. If you had a fever, you didn't receive chemo that week and thereby extending the amount of time to receive treatment. I had a kitten that I needed to get declawed because she could scratch me and cause an infection. I hated doing that to my little cat. Now she hates going to the vet and does everything she can to get out of going.

The second round of chemotherapy had different side effects. I also needed IV Benadryl along with the chemo. It was twenty-five milligrams of IV. The nurse administering it said

I would sleep. "Oh no, twenty-five milligrams won't do that." Fifteen minutes after receiving the Benadryl, I fell asleep. The nurse and my mother had a good laugh. While receiving this round, I needed transportation on treatment day. My brother would drive me to work, and my mother would pick me up, take me to chemo and drive home. We would stop off at a local convenience store that sold turkey dinners with filling, mashed potatoes, green beans, and baked apples. Wonderful food enough for two meals.

I did experience an illness episode. A molar was bothering me, the dentist thought I needed a new filling and replaced an old one. But then I felt chills and still had tooth pain. I had an abscess in my molar. There was a crack in the tooth. I had a fever of 102. I went to the emergency room where they gave me a strong antibiotic, and I returned home with the promise to go to my oncologist the next day, or back to the emergency room for a second dose of the antibiotic. I went to the oncology clinic for the second dose. I contacted my dentist who referred me to a dental surgeon. The dental surgeon pulled my tooth. My friend, Marta, in El Salvador said she also needed to have teeth pulled due to infection (abscess) while receiving chemotherapy. The chemo caused cataracts to develop, that was scary, having my eyesight change quickly. I got a new pair of glasses, only to go back to the eye doctor a month later and needed another pair. Time to see the eye specialist. After the chemotherapy and radiation treatments were completed, I needed cataract surgery. Now my vision has been corrected. I no longer need glasses for distance, just reading. I enjoy going into the dollar stores and buying different frames from one to ten dollars, not four hundred dollars for new glasses. Also, I developed neuropathy (numbness) in my toes and fingertips. Over time it has diminished, however, it is still there. As a nurse, I had a difficult time trying to take a radial pulse (wrist). I need to listen to the heart with a stethoscope.

After finishing the course of chemotherapy, I needed to wait a month before starting radiation. Initially, they took measurements, it took a long time. They made a piece of foam to conform to your body, had to have my arms in a certain position and the foam helped to keep them in place. I hated receiving the radiation treatments. You had to lie very still. The radiation technicians would say, "Don't move." I called them my torturers, only half in jest. Radiation was scheduled every Monday through Friday. The radiation also caused fatigue. During the holidays, they scheduled some Saturday visits. My Christmas present was finishing the treatments. I was scheduled for thirty-three and only needed to receive thirty treatments. Woo-hoo! Thank you, Lord.

The doctors told me it would take a year or more to bounce back from the chemo and radiation. They were right. I continued needing sleep, rest, but slowly, my energy level increased. After going through the mastectomy, chemotherapy, and radiation, I needed to wait and recover for a year before considering reconstruction surgery. After going through all of that and cataract surgery, I decided not to have reconstruction at this time. A coworker also had breast cancer several months after mine. She is in her thirties and decided to have reconstruction done on both her breasts.

Going through the breast cancer, surgery and treatment was an emotional rollercoaster. I cried and called out to God. This was another level of dependency on God that I needed to learn. I had a good friend named Marsha who also had cancer. She had hers for several years before the Lord called her home to Him last year at the age of sixty-two. I would talk to her of my feelings and fears. Marsha stated that I will have thoughts of cancer in the future when I experience twinges or pain. She was right, I do wonder if I have cancer in another part of my body when I feel something different. I could never have gone through all of this without God. Jesus is our rock. No matter the outcome, He is always there. I know that when the time comes, I will be in heaven with my Lord and the loved ones who preceded me.

I have a friend in El Salvador whom I met in the Philippines. Marta is a dentist. We spent a lot of time together while I lived in El Salvador. Marta also had breast cancer, both breasts. She had a double mastectomy. Marta was only in her forties when diagnosed with stage four cancer. She would tell me via email that during chemo, she wanted to give up, but her family encouraged her to continue and she finished the treatment. Marta has given her testimony in several churches. Recently, she attended a survivor's party, five years since the mastectomy and treatment. One of her doctors was there. He said, "How can you be here? You should have died from the cancer."

Marta replied, "Only through God, He has healed me." Her story encourages me.

I had my yearly checkup with the radiation oncologist (the other oncologist I see three times a year now) in August. She told me I looked well and that I have survived two and a half years since finishing treatment; with God's help, I will make it through the next two and a half years to become a five-year survivor like Marta.

There are many areas of healing, not just physical, but emotional and spiritual as well. God is there for us in our struggles and sufferings. Psalm 23 (NLT) states, "The Lord is my shepherd, I have all that I need. He lets me rest in green meadows; he leads me beside peaceful streams. He renews my strength. He guides me along right paths, bringing honor to his name. Even when I walk through the darkest valley, I will not be afraid, for you are close beside me. Your rod and your staff protect and comfort me. You prepare a feast for me in the presence of my enemies. You honor me by anointing my head with oil. My cup overflows with blessings. Surely your goodness and unfailing love will pursue me all the days of my life, and I will live in the house of the Lord forever." God cares about our problems, concerns, illnesses. He can heal us supernaturally, performs miracles (yes, this still happens), gradual healing—if physical, maybe you need surgery, chemotherapy, medication, therapy and time but the healing occurs. If you need healing emotionally or spiritually, God will show you His love in numerous ways, through a friend, family member, or nature. Emotional wounds take time, but gradually the pain lessens. The ultimate healing is when we go to be with our Lord. We receive a new body, no more pain or sorrow. Turn to our Lord when you hurt. Tell Him your feelings. Psalm 34:18 (NLT) states, "The Lord is close to the brokenhearted. He rescues those whose spirit is crushed."

The Lord has given us His word to read and learn more about Him. Please take the time to read His book. You may want to have a devotional reading or read the Bible in a year program. There are Bible apps for both with daily reminders on your cell phones. When you find yourself caught up in situations, work, fatigue, and realize you haven't read your Bible in several weeks, please don't feel like you must read all of the days you missed. Talk to our Lord, then pick up the reading for today. Sometimes we feel we have to earn God's love, but God's love is a gift to us. You may prefer to be involved in a Bible study at church or someone's home. There are even groups who have teleconference Bible studies. I take part in one of these. The people online are from all over the country—Montana, Texas, Ohio, Michigan, Georgia, Maryland, and other places. Most of the people I haven't met, but I call them and talk and pray with them because of what we share during the Bible study. The teleconference was a blessing for me. A friend told me about it while I was recovering from chemotherapy and radiation. Having fellowship with other believers is important, whether it is church services, Bible studies, or getting together for dinner and a movie. Enjoy each other's company and lift up the name of Jesus. Tell them what He has done for you recently.

Now my brother and I are dealing with our mother's health. We were told she was pre-Alzheimer, but there was a big change in her personality, after having surgery on the sac surrounding her heart a year ago. She has, at times, refused help from us, refused to eat or drink. Mom has developed urinary tract infections throughout this past year, as well as having her blood levels not being within normal range as a result of not drinking enough. Mom would also refuse help from a visiting nurse at times. Finally, Medicare agreed to rehabilitation for thirty days to help Mom gain strength after the most recent hospitalization. However, the doctor at the nursing home told us Mom has vascular dementia, small blood vessels being shut off in her brain probably from blood clots from the surgery. The doctor started her on a second antidepressant which has definitely helped. Mother has improved. She wants to be home. The doctor says she needs 24/7 care. My brother who lives next door to Mom has moved in with her. She has some good days and not so good days. I'm grateful my brother is willing to try this arrangement. She has been home for six weeks now. We are praying that Mom can enjoy life. Saturday she was talking about buying birdseed for the birds and squirrels this winter, which she always enjoyed.

Caretaking is stressful. There are many things to do and consider. Stress for the main caretaker. Financial issues. Power of attorney, my brother and I are both her powers of attorney. Looking into assisted living, does he/she qualify, or if necessary, back to a skilled nursing home. I've visited a few facilities and continue getting calls by these facilities to see how Mom is doing and have we made any decisions yet. Consider contacting an agency that would help with bathing and housekeeping. Buying food, paying bills, plus caretaker needing to take care of his/her needs and bills. I've worked with the elderly in the past. It is more difficult working with your parent than another person. Please pray for our entire family, mother, my brother and his family, and myself. Thank you.

MISSIONS

While growing up, I remember listening to missionaries who visited our church. Their stories fascinated me, how the people lived and how God used the missionaries to help the people, and for them to learn about Jesus and accept Him as their Lord and Savior. My parents also had ordered a monthly series of booklets about different countries around the world. I looked through these books a while back, countries that no longer exist such as Yugoslavia, or been renamed such as British Honduras is now Belize. Since then I've been interested in different cultures. I believe these experiences helped to shape me, and lead me into a desire to serve as a missionary. What I didn't realize was my missionary experiences to different countries wouldn't start until I was thirty-nine. The Lord can call you at any time in your life to be a missionary. One church I worked with on a trip to El Salvador, there were two older ladies in their seventies. "This is our first trip, we know we are meant to be here, but don't know why." The ladies brought small toys for the children, face painting supplies, and Polaroid cameras. For many of the children, this was their first encounter with medical people, doctors, and nurses. The lead doctor who had led numerous mission trips prior to this one stated this was the best trip due in part to the ladies ministering to the children. They were not afraid to see the doctors. It was a fun atmosphere. One of my trips to Peru, we had an area for children to attend while their parents were being seen by the medical team. They had little activities; arts and crafts, stickers, which the children enjoyed.

This is definitely a ministry area. You may think you don't have any special skills, but there are many ways to help out on mission trips. My church went to a mountain town in Nicaragua for a week. There was only one day I went to a local clinic to help. The other days I helped paint with a long roller and talked with the children who came by after school. There are many ways to serve. You will bless people and receive more blessings as a result of obeying God and attending the trips.

Nicaraguan Mountain.

If you are planning to go on a short-term mission trip with your church or another organization, check to see what is required before going. Passport, is it up-to-date? Make a second copy in case the original becomes misplaced or lost. Vaccines, when was your last tetanus? Contact your doctor's office, see if you need a booster. Hepatitis A, this is the form of hepatitis that is fecal-oral route. I know, gross, but someone may work in the fields with the vegetables, use the facilities, and not wash their hands or unable to wash their hands. You might eat that food, protect yourself and get Hepatitis A vaccine. In the USA, many doctors now recommend Hepatitis A vaccine for school-aged children. You may be going to a country that has yellow fever or typhoid, there are vaccines for these. Malaria is in tropical countries, for this you take an oral medicine starting prior to the trip. Check the government travel site for any travel restrictions and vaccine suggestions for the country you are going to.

Other medicines and supplements to take with you: calcium, you may not be getting dairy products and may experience leg cramps, take a calcium supplement, also a multivitamin. Also take with you Acetaminophen, Ibuprofen, for pain, fever. Bismuth and Loperamide tablets for diarrhea and nausea. If you take prescription drugs, keep them in their original bottles in case you are selected at the airport for a search. Also, keep them in your carry-on luggage.

Other items to take with you: toilet paper, yes, they have it at the hotel but maybe not at the work site; washcloths—some hotels only provide towels; hand sanitizer; favorite snacks; granola bars; peanut butter; jerky for protein; Gatorade powder to put in your water bottle, both for flavor and to replenish your electrolytes. On one trip, there was a baby with diarrhea, another nurse borrowed my Gatorade powder and gave the baby a bottle. Shampoo, conditioner, small bottle of liquid detergent or dishwashing soap to wash your clothes if laundry facilities are not provided. Rag rugs you can buy at a dollar store to use for a bath mat. When your trip is finished, you can leave some of the items in the hotel for the maids, providing them blessings. Many people can't afford shampoo, so this is a treat. Or if you are working with missionaries, they could put the items to good use. Also, you may want to bless the missionaries by bringing things they want or miss, maybe puzzle books, reading books, magazines, candy, or food, they need ministering to also.

Do not take with you gold or other expensive jewelry; you may be targeted for robbery or worse.

If you are going on a long flight and are over forty, and/or obese, please purchase for yourself some TED stockings (these are compression stockings and help with circulation and try to prevent blood clots from forming), also do some leg and foot exercises while sitting on the plane.

For those of you who are being led into long-term missions, please consider what is involved. If you are going to a country that doesn't have English as their primary language, you will need to attend classes; if it is not a romance language such as Spanish, French, German, or Italian, then it becomes more difficult to learn. However, if you are being led by the Lord to go to a country in Africa or Asia, then He will provide you with the ability to learn the language. Fundraising, you need money to live wherever you go, and to provide for transportation, also for trips back home. I was blessed in that I lived with my mother for several years and saved some money. I had in my mind an amount to spend during the two years I lived in El Salvador. Also, I was blessed with the church school I taught at, providing me an apartment and four hundred dollars a month. I also taught at a language school evenings and Saturdays for extra money. I did talk to some churches that I attended throughout the years, two churches provided me monthly funding of one hundred fifty dollars.

Personally, I have a difficult time asking for money, so the Lord provided for me by having me live with my mother to save money. However, you may need to ask for funding from friends, churches, family. Again, the Lord will provide for you and give you the abilities to request funding. Insurance—you may want to obtain travelers' insurance while you are a missionary, or some church denominations will cover you with their insurance. Some people are able to cover themselves with their own insurance, perhaps with COBRA. You will need to consider insurance in the case of becoming ill and needing medical attention either in-country or back home in the USA.

Research the area of your mission focus. Check out their customs, clothing needs, foods. Visit restaurants in the States that serve this type of food. Bring plenty of medication with you. Also, bring a laptop to communicate with family, friends, churches, and supporters back home.

These are just some of many possible mission/ministry areas. Perhaps you may want to provide your church or community with another service such as providing rides to doctor appointments for people who can't drive; or arrange to take people grocery shopping. Another suggestion is cleaning and organizing someone's house or apartment. Please keep in mind the person may feel embarrassed with how messy the house is. Show God's love to them, don't pass judgment. Many people do not want strangers in their house; they may be more receptive of help from someone in their church or neighborhood.

You will learn many things during your time as a missionary. When I first moved to El Salvador, I stayed with another lady from the school until an apartment was found. I was told by friends that I needed to throw a party. When something good happens, you throw a party. I invited people from previous mission trips and from school. I made some American dishes—Boston baked beans, pasta Alfredo, honey- mustard chicken, and set the time for 6:00 p.m. At 6:15 p.m., two friends arrived. After visiting for twenty minutes, I asked, "Where is everyone?"

"Oh, they will be here between 7:00 and 7:30 p.m."

Sure enough, people arrived during that time. Also, during the party, I learned I should have coffee on hand. I'm not a coffee drinker. One of the dentists said, "I would like some coffee."

"I'm sorry, I don't have any."

"But I would really like some coffee."

"I'm sorry, I don't have any. I have iced tea and hot tea, soda, and juice, but no coffee." My friend was disappointed.

You could be entertaining someone and accidentally offend them. If you are going to a Latin American country, have a jar of instant coffee on hand if you don't drink it. Or, if you are being led to an Asian country, perhaps you will need to have tea available.

Before committing yourself to a long-term mission, please take the time to visit the country of interest. Meet other missionaries. Ask about their experiences and any suggestions they have for you to prepare yourself, or items to bring with you. When you do become a long-term missionary, take time to get together with other missionaries for supper and support. Pray together.

If you want to do missions in the USA, there are organizations that you can inquire about, here are a few: Convoy of Hope, Habitat for Humanity, Mission of Mercy, Operation Blessing, Samaritan's Purse. Please also consider home missions. There are many "mission" opportunities to minister to others. Local food banks, nursing homes, assisted living homes, women's shelters, rescue missions, after- school programs, organizations helping disabled veterans, hospitals, prisons. Give time to caregivers, relieve the caregiver for two to three hours so they could go to the store, the beauty shop, or just take a nap.

Bless someone with a surprise—supper, movie tickets, gift certificates for shopping, or special treats like a manicure. You can even have a little fun and be anonymous.

Looking back over my life, seeing what I've been through, I'm so glad to have known the Lord. There is no way on my own that I could handle these situations. I pray this book has touched your heart and brings you closer to our Lord. Hopefully, you can look back on your life, and see how God has brought you through. Take time to enjoy just being in His presence. "Be still and know that I am God" (Ps. 46:10, NASB). If you need to cry out to God for help or forgiveness, He will provide. If you have never asked the Lord into your life, you can do so now.

Pastor J.D. Farag of Calvary Chapel Kaneohe, on the island of Maui, Hawaii, has listed the ABCs of salvation.

A. Admit you are a sinner. (A sin is doing something wrong. Maybe you lied to your parents at some point, and if that was the only sin you've ever committed, it is still a sin and separates you from God.) Romans 3:10 (NASB) states, "There is none righteous, not even one." Romans 3:23 (NASB) states, "For all have sinned and fallen short of the glory of God." Jesus came to earth, lived a sinless life and died on the cross with all of our sins on Him, so we could be restored to God.

B. Believe in the Lord Jesus Christ.

C. Confess with your mouth that Jesus is Lord. Romans 10: 9–11 states, "That if you confess with your mouth Jesus as Lord, and believe in your heart that God raised Him from the dead, you will be saved; for with the heart a person believes resulting in righteousness and with the mouth he confesses resulting in salvation." Romans 3:13

states, "Whoever will call on the name of the Lord will be saved."

One day soon, our Lord will return and I look forward to meeting you, and celebrating with you, our going home to be with Jesus.

QUESTIONS

Now for the hard part for you, below are some questions to ask yourself. If you are like me, I write what pops into my head. But after you do that, please take the time to ponder the questions. Ask God to show things He has done for you during your lifetime.

Look back on your family through the generations, what has happened or not happened that you are here today?

Looking at your childhood experiences both positive and negative, how has that shaped you today? Can you see God's hand of protection?

Look at your teenage and young adult years, your decisions both good and not so good. Did you pray during these times? Do you have family who prayed for you?

How has God surprised you? As you've read, one of my surprises were all the people who supported me during my breast cancer, people who didn't even know me.

We all have a tendency to put ourselves down. I call myself stupid frequently (which I need to stop). I make mistakes. We have been given gifts, talents, abilities.

Try to list ten positive things about yourself, then get together with a good friend. Have your friend tell you positive traits that they see in you. Add these to your list, post it on the bathroom mirror, and repeat them daily to yourself. You are an awesome person.

How is your support system? Do you try to do everything yourself? Who can you ask for help during a crisis, or dealing with an elderly loved one? In your area, what programs are offered through the Area Agency on Aging? Can you name a situation where you know God intervened for you? Protected you? Have you ever been late leaving for work only to see an accident and think, "If I left on time, I may have been in that accident."

Take time for yourself, we all need to rest.

Consider starting a prayer journal. Write down people you pray for, any specific needs, and later how God answered the prayers.

Surrender Your Struggles to God

Al Divino Salvador del Mundo. The divine Savior of the World statue in San Salvador, El Salvador.

Leesa King

My friend Marta and her family.

ABOUT THE AUTHOR

Leesa King is a registered nurse, who has worked in mental health settings with individuals of all ages, and also as a school nurse. She enjoys helping people and learning about other cultures. Leesa has participated in short-term mission trips to El Salvador, Nicaragua, Peru, and the Philippines. She went to El Salvador as a teacher at a bilingual Christian school. She taught grades three and four during the mornings, and eleventh grade English in the afternoons for two years. During this time, El Salvador experienced two major earthquakes. Leesa volunteered at the Salvadoran Red Cross until the schools reopened.

    Leesa is also a breast cancer survivor of three years. She is grateful to God for His love, mercy, protection, and provisions. She is thankful for the family and friends God blessed her with. Leesa was encouraged to write her life story by Rev. Charlotte Holliday who has been a wonderful friend for thirty years.

www.ingramcontent.com/pod-product-compliance
Lightning Source LLC
Chambersburg PA
CBHW071507070526
44578CB00001B/463